Course Creation

5-Day Complete Course Creation Guide

By

Amanda Rose

Day 1: Topic

The first step is building your course is choosing a topic!

Brainstorming

What are you good at? What do you know that you'd enjoy teaching? What skill do you have that you think others could benefit from? List everything that comes to mind: _____

_____

_____

_____

_____

_____

_____

_____

_____

_____

_____

_____

_____

After brainstorming you've most likely discovered that you have a TON of topics that you could teach. Eventually, you may wish to create courses for all of them, but for now, you need to choose one. How do you do that?

Market Research

What's the best way to determine what to teach? Ask your audience. See what your following wants to learn; by asking them you ensure the course you create will be in high demand when you launch!

Narrow down your topics to 2-4 you're very excited about that you think your niche market will be interested in and pose the questions (this can be on social media or to your e-mail list) asking which they are most interested in learning.

My Market Research Feedback was _____

_____

_____

_____

_____

_____

_____

_____

No Market to Ask Yet?

What are the best ways for me to build my audience?

_____

_____

_____

_____

_____

_____

_____

_____

_____

_____

_____

_____

_____

_____

_____

Confidence

Confidence is paramount to being able to move forward with your course creation and then being able to sell it. Creating your course is going to help a lot of people. It's our duty when we learn something to pass that knowledge on to help our fellow human being.

Paying forward what you know is so important; it's how we all get to grow! Now you're going to pledge to teach your knowledge!

Pledge

I, _____, am great at _____ and I realize that I am only _____ in _____ people who find this easy! It is my duty to teach this to help others! I Pledge to create my course so that I can help others learn this amazing skill and improve their lives!

Decision

Make your choice. What is your course topic? Don't put off choosing this. You can create more courses, and do so with ease, after completing this process. Pick you topic now, commit to it, and learn this course building process.

I have chosen to create my course around the topic of _____

_____

_____

Day 2: The Pitch

It's time to work on the sales copy for your course; this will be the basis for everything you create and how you market it!

Brainstorming Ideas

To create your sales copy, you'll first want to point form your ideas for each part of your message. This will enable you to write with clarity and ease.

My Ideal Client's Pain Points Are: _____

_____

_____

_____

_____

_____

_____

_____

_____

_____

My Ideal Client Desires: _____

_____

_____

_____

_____

_____

_____

I'm Relatable Because: _____

_____

_____

_____

_____

_____

_____

_____

The Solution for my Ideal Client is: _____

_____

_____

_____

_____

_____

_____

_____

The Next Step My Ideal Client Needs to Take Is: _____

_____

_____

_____

Which Means my Call Take Action Should Be: _____

_____

_____

_____

_____

Putting it Together

Practice writing sales copy. Keep in mind that you're writing it to your niche market; keep the focus on their needs and your words will not only flow out but be full of meaning! Once you've written up sales copy that makes you go, "Wow! I'd buy that in a heartbeat!" then you've got the right one!

_____

_____

_____

_____

_____

_____

_____

_____

_____

_____

_____

_____

_____

_____

_____

_____

_____

_____

_____

_____

_____

_____

_____

_____

_____

_____

_____

_____

Day 3: The Layout

Now it's time to give your course structure. By giving your course it's layout, you'll then be able to easily fill in the content.

First of all, you need to determine how long your course will be. There is no "Right Answer" for length, however there are some ways to decide what's the best option for your course. Most courses range from 3 days to 1-month. Beyond 1-month in length often participation attendance drops. Answer the following question to gain insight on the ideal length of your course:

*Do I want to impart condensed information or dig deep into each theme beneath my main topic?*_____

_____

_____

*How much information do I have to share?*_____

_____

_____

Am I trying to instill a new habit in my participants?

_____

How many sub-topics do I have to elaborate on? _____

_____

_____

_____

_____

Am I offering to incorporate 1:1 help along with the course material? _____

_____

_____

_____

If you're focused on just a few main points and expanding on them, a 3-7-day time frame will suffice.

If you have a lot of information to cover, figure out all of your main sub-topics; each sub-topic = 1 day. Your clients need time to go through and digest this new information, so sticking to 1 main theme per day will help them to learn and apply the information.

If you're attempting to instill a new habit in your attendees, you'll want to aim for 3 weeks (it takes 3 weeks to establish a new habit).

If you want a course that will submerse your attendees and help them have a transformation from day one until the last day, aim for a 1-month program. Change takes time, and this gives them the time to learn, apply, and see change.

If you're offering 1:1 as a part of your course, you'll need to take into account how much time you'll need to work with each person, how many people will attend, and when you'll work that into your course.

Your Layout

Step 1: Review your Sales Copy

Day 2: Point Form Ideas

- _____
- _____
- _____
- _____
- _____
- _____
- _____
- _____
- _____
- _____
- _____
- _____
- _____
- _____
- _____

Step 3: Create Headings and Subheadings

_____

_____

_____

_____

_____

_____

_____

_____

_____

_____

_____

_____

_____

_____

_____

_____

_____

_____

_____

_____

_____

_____

_____

_____

_____

_____

_____

_____

_____

_____

_____

_____

_____

_____

_____

_____

_____

_____

_____

_____

_____

_____

_____

_____

_____

_____

_____

_____

_____

_____

_____

_____

_____

_____

_____

_____

_____

_____

_____

_____

_____

_____

_____

_____

_____

Day 4: The Content

Now it's time to create your content! You've got your structure, now it's just about sharing your knowledge! We're going to take your headings and sub headings and begin to fill in those sections with your incredible teachings.

Think of all of the things you've learned about this topic. Imagine the person you're teaching is there with you and you're guiding them through it; this will help you think in a step-by-step approach. Most of all, don't overthink this just let it flow – you can edit and reword it all later. Get all of your amazing knowledge out on the page, we'll perfect it later.

Now, let's start creating content!

MAIN HEADING _____

SUBHEADING _____

_____

_____

_____

_____

_____

_____

_____

_____

_____

_____

_____

_____

_____

_____

_____

_____

_____

_____

_____

SUBHEADING

SUBHEADING _____

SUBHEADING_____

SUBHEADING_____

MAIN HEADING _____
SUBHEADING _____

_____

_____

_____

_____

_____

_____

_____

_____

_____

_____

_____

_____

_____

_____

_____

_____

_____

_____

_____

_____

_____

SUBHEADING_____

_____

_____

_____

_____

_____

_____

_____

_____

_____

_____

_____

_____

_____

_____

_____

_____

_____

_____

_____

_____

_____

_____

SUBHEADING_____

_____

_____

_____

_____

_____

_____

_____

_____

_____

_____

_____

_____

_____

_____

_____

_____

_____

_____

_____

_____

_____

_____

SUBHEADING_____

_____

_____

_____

_____

_____

_____

_____

_____

_____

_____

_____

_____

_____

_____

_____

_____

_____

_____

_____

_____

SUBHEADING_____

_____

_____

_____

_____

_____

_____

_____

_____

_____

_____

_____

_____

_____

_____

_____

_____

_____

_____

_____

_____

_____

_____

MAIN HEADING _____
SUBHEADING _____

_____

_____

_____

_____

_____

_____

_____

_____

_____

_____

_____

_____

_____

_____

_____

_____

_____

_____

_____

SUBHEADING

SUBHEADING_____

_____

_____

_____

_____

_____

_____

_____

_____

_____

_____

_____

_____

_____

_____

_____

_____

_____

_____

_____

_____

_____

SUBHEADING

SUBHEADING_____

Video Content

Point form notes for my videos:

Day 1:

_____

_____

_____

_____

_____

_____

_____

_____

_____

_____

_____

_____

_____

_____

Day 2:

_____

_____

_____

_____

_____

_____

_____

_____

_____

_____

_____

_____

_____

_____

_____

_____

Day 3:

_____

_____

_____

_____

_____

_____

_____

_____

_____

_____

_____

_____

_____

_____

_____

_____

_____

Companion Workbook

Do I want to create a companion for this course? _____
If you choose yes, here's how:

1. Create all of your course content first.
2. Open up a new Word Doc to use as your Workbook
3. If you want to use a background image like I do in my workbooks, get the image you want to use (make sure it's royalty free or that you've paid for it) and go to DESIGN > WATERMARK > CUSTOM WATERMARK and then upload your image
4. Set up your workbook to mirror your written training (you can use the same headings/subheadings)
5. Help the take action or solidify their knowledge by giving them workspace and asking questions related to what they learned from the written or video trainings
6. Under the subheadings have space for them to
   a. Write out the work
   b. Answer questions
   c. Take notes

Types of Learning

People fall into 3 main types when it comes to how we learn: Visual, Auditory, and Kinesthetic.

Visual learners learn best through what they see. Reading and watching help them best.

Auditory learners learn best through what they hear. Audio recordings and videos help them learn best.

Kinesthetic learners learn best through what they feel. Hands on and applying what they are taught helps them learn best.

Keep this in mind as you craft your course; it will help you to ensure you incorporate various ways of expressing your ideas, so all of your participants benefit!

Day 5: Market and Sell your Course!

You've just created your course, now it's time to sell it!

Pricing

Deciding on the price tag

Course Length

How many days is the course? _____

How much involvement per day? (Are they going to be showing up with you from sun-up to sun-down or will they just show up 30-60 minutes a day?) _____

_____

_____

What value are you providing? _____

_____

_____

_____

What transformation will your participants get? _____

_____

_____

_____

When you think about the price what price feels scary~ big and makes you think, "Ugh, that's too much!" and likewise, which price feels undervaluing your content making you think, "I'd resent showing up for this pittance." The right price will fall between these two numbers.

What price feels like too much? _____

What price would you begrudge getting? _____

What's the median price between the 'too high' and 'too low'? _____

How does this price feel? _____

What you FEEL about your price is what your prospects will feel about it.

If you feel you're charging to much, so will your prospects, and they won't buy it. The energy with which you place behind you number is the energy your buyers will feel. Likewise, if you charge too little energetically, your prospects might wonder, "Why so little? Is this worth it?" if you feel like it's undervalued. What you feel they feel.

Only you know the right price for your course. My rule of thumb? I always give more value in transformation than I ask for in money. This feels good for me and for my clients.

Sales Copy

Surprise! You already have your sales copy from Day 2 when you created your pitch! If you added more goodness to your course you want to highlight, add it to your pitch, but otherwise? You're good to go!

Niche

Who is this course for? Answer the following questions to gain clarity on who your ideal audience is!

How old are they? _____

Are they single or married? _____

Where do they live? _____

Do they rent or own their home? _____

What's most important to them? _____

_____

_____

What fears do they have? _____

_____

_____

_____

Are they an introvert or extravert? _____

Are they parents, want to be parents, or don't want kids? _____

_____

_____

_____

Do they have a job? _____

What do they like to spend their time doing? _____

_____

_____

_____

What are their aspirations? _____

_____

_____

_____

What do they have a hard time with? _____

_____

_____

_____

Do they have a sense of humor? _____

_____

_____

_____

Are they a perfectionist? _____

_____

_____

_____

Have they started working on their dream yet? _____

_____

_____

_____

Are they more visual, audio, or kinesthetic? _____

_____

_____

_____

Getting the Word Out

- Get in front of Your Niche
  - You now have an idea of your Niche Market's interests, so get yourself in front of them by joining social media groups and using hashtags related to those interests
- Social Media
  - Start posting about your upcoming course on social media
  - Do LIVE videos discussing your upcoming course
  - Give value related to the course topic to wet your audiences' appetite
- E-mail
  - If you already have an e-mail list, then send out an e-mail telling them about the course
  - If your don't yet have an e-mail list start to collect e-mails (you can use a free
- Free Advertising
  - Blogs
  - Podcasts
  - Newspapers
  - Radio

Talking to People

I will focus on cultivating relationships with my niche market. I will engage in _____ new conversations every day.

Follow-Up

Following up is imperative to making sales. I will follow up with interested prospects at least _____ times.

NOTES

_____

_____

_____

_____

_____

_____

_____

_____

_____

_____

_____

_____

_____

_____

_____

_____

_____

_____

_____

_____

_____

_____

_____

Amanda Rose

_____
_____
_____
_____
_____
_____
_____
_____
_____
_____
_____
_____
_____
_____
_____
_____
_____
_____
_____
_____
_____
_____
_____
_____

_____

_____

_____

_____

_____

_____

_____

_____

_____

_____

_____

_____

_____

_____

_____

_____

_____

_____

_____

_____

_____

_____

_____

_____

A Few of Amanda's Other Courses...

Master your mindset and you master your life! The key to success, wealth, happiness, health, and all of the good things you WANT in your life are unlocked through your mindset!

In this special 90-Minute Mastermind I will teach you...

🌙 How your thoughts have been dictating your results

🌙 Why mastering your mindset is the key to your success

🌙 Why you are where you are based on your past conditioning

🌙 How to reprogram your mind to support you in creating the life you've always wanted

🌙 How to retrain your mind to support you instead of hinder you

🌙 How you can have MORE fun and make MORE money while you Work LESS

🌙 And much more...

A 90-Minute session with me would normally cost $375, but for this Mindset Mastery 90-Minute Mastermind you're going to get in for JUST $11!!!

Contact Amanda to Gain Access
Amanda@AmandaRoseFitness.com

This is a 5-Day workshop that will take you through everything from how to choose your topic, structure your course, create content, and how to market and sell it!

In 5-Days You'll have ALL of the skills you need to create and launch your course!

You're going to get...

✿ The #1 Insider Secret to Creating a Course that Sells VS one That Flops

✿ Step-By-Step walk-through on creating your course from concept to launch

✿ Daily Video Training

✿ Daily Written Training

✿ 1:1 Messenger and Voice Message Access to Amanda for Individual Help

✿ Launch Strategies

✿ Course Creation Workbook PDF

Are you ready to create your course, help others learn, and expand your biz?! Let's do this!

This 5-Day workshop is just $222. Register Here:
https://amanda-rose.mykajabi.com/offers/RLeeQAhF

This 90-Minute Mastermind is going to give you all the skills you need to master sales and enjoy making them!

In Sales Mastery I'm going to teach you...

👽 What sales REALLY are (it's not what you think!)

👽 To Understand what GOOD sales transactions feel like

👽 The Importance of Value in Sales

👽 How to create a deep seeded belief in your Product or Service

👽 How to Start a Sales Conversation

👽 Easily and Effortlessly Handling Objections

👽 The Importance of the Follow Up

👽 How to Ask For the Sale

👽 Closing the Sale in a Way That Has you and your New Customer Jumping For Joy

And much more!!!

You're also going to get 🎁:

The Sales Marketing Workbook!

It's time to turn your passion into profit and HAVE FUN doing it!

Learn more and Sign Up to Save Your Spot Here!
https://amanda-rose.mykajabi.com/offers/SoLTh5xc

It's time to make Sales Fun!

In the Money Mastery 90-Minute Mindset Gurus, Xerces A Lewis Your Intuitive Soul Doctor, and Amanda Rose Mindset Coach & Author of the Manifesting Series will help you...

💰 To heal your relationship with money so that you naturally begin to attract it

💰 To understand the true meaning of wealth and abundance so that you aren't subconsciously repelling it

💰 Learn what they NEVER taught you in school about wealth creation

💰 Understand how the rich think differently from the poor & the middle class

💰 To get into the energetic flow of money so that you become a money magnet!

95% of wealthy people started with nothing. That means YOU can too!

We're going to show you the path, the only question is... are you ready to walk it?

A 90-Minute session with Myself and Xerces would normally cost $565, but for this Mindset Mastery 90-Minute Mastermind you're going to get in for JUST $88!

Contact Amanda to Gain Access
Amanda@AmandaRoseFitness.com

This course is going to cover everything from the writing process, to editing, formatting, and publishing, and how to successfully market your book. what works and how to do it properly, and what to avoid. It's compiling over a year's worth of research, so you don't have to spend endless hours trying to figure out what to do to get your book recognized, in the press, into bookstores, libraries, and land book signings.

If you're ready to finally write your book, get it out in the world, and generate an incredible income through book royalties, then it's time to sign up for this 3-week online workshop!

Learn More:
https://amanda-rose.mykajabi.com/offers/7bUzKNX2/checkout

About the Author

Amanda Rose is an avid reader and storyteller. Working in a variety of mediums and genres, communicating new ways of thinking is her passion.

Amanda works as an online Health and Fitness coach, Mindset & Business Coach, Actor, Model, Motivational Speaker, Online Course Creator and Writer.

Residing in Kingston, Ontario, with her husband and 3 cats, Amanda is currently working on her next novel. Get in touch with Amanda by visiting her website:

HTTPS://Amanda-rose.mykajabi.com

Manifesting Your Best Life

Manifesting Your Best Life Book Description:

Stop dreaming about a better life and start living it!

Manifesting You Best Life is going to show you that "Living Your Best Life" isn't just some cute meme on social media – it can be your way of life! The 21 nugget-of-wisdom chapters in this self-help book are for people who want to start living their best life, but don't know where to begin. It will give you the skills to take you from dreaming about your best life, to making it your reality!

You will learn:
•How to Identify what living your best life really means to you.
•The steps needed to stop wishing and start living your best life.
•How to use the Law of Attraction to support your efforts.
•Successful habits that will change your life.
•And how to create the life you've always wanted... And start living it NOW!

By the end of Manifesting Your Best Life, you will have a clear picture of what your dream life looks like, how to get there, and the tools and skills to make it into your reality!

Are you ready to begin?

ALSO AVAILABLE ON AUDIBLE

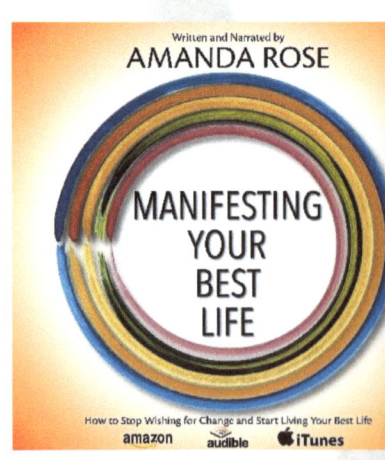

The Manifesting 30-Day Guided Journal

From the author of Manifesting on Purpose comes The Manifesting 30-Day Guided Journal!

This Law of Attraction Based Journal will take your Manifesting Practice to The Next Level!

The Manifesting 30-Day Guided Journal will walk you through 30 days of curated activities that will get you into the energetic flow of manifestation. Through goal-setting, mindfulness, clarity, and actionable steps, you will learn how to create the life of happiness and freedom that you've always desired.

The Orgasmic Cookbook

The Orgasmic Cookbook Book Description:

Nutrition Meets Flavor.

Just because it's healthy doesn't mean it should be boring. In *The Orgasmic Cookbook* Amanda teaches her best tips and tricks to make healthy food pop with flavor! Having lost over 100 pounds Amanda knows the importance of eating healthy. As a food lover she's made it her mission to create healthy recipes packed with rich taste!

Get ready for mouth-watering recipes that will give you a whole new appreciation for food!

Manifesting on Purpose

Manifesting on Purpose Book Description:

It's time to take manifesting off auto-pilot, get behind the wheel, and start steering your life in the direction you want it to go!

Manifesting on Purpose clarifies why we manifest what we do, why we experience the same things over and over again, until we step in and weed out our own mental gardens.

Ever wonder how is it that 2 people can start off with the same opportunity, and one will become a massive success, while the other barely scrapes by? What's the defining factor?

What do successful people know that we're missing? We've been taught that the harder we work the more money, happiness, and success we'll have in life; but if this was the case successful people would constantly we run ragged, and be bleary eyed from lack of sleep, instead of enjoying lots of free time pursuing their heart's desires. So, what are we missing?

The Law of Attraction is always working, even when we're not focused on it. The Law of Attraction states that, "Like Attracts Like," we are all energy, so our thoughts get reflected back to us. Your thoughts create your physical reality. The problem? We're always thinking! Our thoughts, ungoverned, bounce around from idea to idea, and all too often, focus on the immediate problems in our lives, creating a feedback loop. Since we attract back what we think about, if we're focused on our problems, what's going to show up? More problems!

Your mind is your most valuable asset. Your thoughts literally create your reality. Your current situation is a reflection of your previous thoughts. Most people, however, do not consciously decide what they want, their subconscious belief systems run everything on auto-pilot; making most people feel as if they are victims of their circumstances. YOU ARE NOT A VICTIM OF CIRCUMSTANCE!

You are in the driver's seat, you simply have to take control of the wheel! Take manifesting off auto-pilot and create the life you want! "But I think positive thoughts," you say. Your conscious thoughts will always be secondary to your subconscious thoughts in the way of manifestation. Until you change your core beliefs to line up with who you wish to become, and what you wish to do, you cannot break the old cycles.

Are you ready to take control? Have abundance in money, love, health, freedom, experiences, and all other areas of your life? Then let's get started!

Manifesting Money: How to Master and Apply Abundance Mindset in Your Life

Manifesting Money Book description: Master Your Mindset and You Master Your Life!

Why does 99% of the population struggle financially? Is it a lack of opportunity? An issue with education? Not having the right skills? Poor investment choices? Bad timing? Low work performance?

The startling answer is: none of the above!

Wealth creation is a mindset.

It's not what rich people *do*, but how they *think* that sets them apart. *Manifesting Money* is going to teach you how to:

•Discover and Get Rid of Money Blocks
•Kick Fear and Doubt to the Curb
•Create New Supportive Money Beliefs
•Develop Wealth Consciousness
•Build Multiple Sources of Income
•Work Smarter Not Harder
•Manage Money
•Implement the Successful Habits Rich People Use
•Have the Wealth You've Always Wanted

It's time to start *Manifesting Money*!

Get Published Workbook: Write | Publish | Market

Get Published Workbook Book Description:

Most people have thought about publishing a book, but the majority will never even begin writing one. Why? The process can seem daunting. Conceptualizing, writing, editing, formatting, copywriting, publishing, and finally marketing; it can seem like an overwhelming amount of work when you aren't sure what each step entails.

In this workbook, you're going to learn all of my best practices so you can go from concept to published in 2-6 months pending on the length and style of your book, with full knowledge of what to expect, and what to do, so nothing will stand in your way of becoming a successful author!

Self-publishing is an incredible avenue to get your work to your readers fast, with widespread distribution, that allows you to take the lion's share of the profits for the book you put all the work into creating!

With self-publishing, you're in control, but that also means you are in charge of your own marketing campaign. Don't let that scare you away! With social media and online sales booming, you can reach your ideal reader audience easier, and at much less cost, than with traditional marketing. You just need to learn how!

Through this book, you're going to learn...
- How to brainstorm and develop a concept
- How to effectively begin writing your book
- How to create disciplined habits to finish your book
- How to edit, format, and polish your book so it's ready for publication
- Why reviews are the life-blood of self-publishing, and how to get them
- How to write an effective book description
- How to write a gripping back cover
- Why your book cover is your most important investment
- How the self-publishing process works
- Best practices for ultimate exposure
- How to use inexpensive pay-per-click campaigns to drive traffic
- Social Media Marketing
- Free marketing practices
- Inexpensive marketing options
- Importance of an author web site to boost SEO
...And much more!

Fire Fury Freedom

"A veritable saga of a dystopian novel by an author with a genuine flair for detailed originality, and narrative driven storytelling, "Fire Fury Freedom" by Amanda Rose is an extraordinary and truly memorable read from cover to cover." -*Midwest Book Review*

Prequel to the Fire Fury Frontier Series

Fire Fury Freedom Book Description:

A dying planet on the verge of collapse.... tormented pasts that haunt the present... an ancient hidden magick...

The C.D.F.P. mega-corporation rules all, with unchecked power, and dark secrets...

The planet is dying, and they are the last hope to save it... Mack, an ex-soldier of the C.D.F.P. military division, and his mercenaries, standalone against the C.D.F.P. (AKA the Company), in the fight for humanities survival. Left unchallenged, the company has ruled over the East Green Continent with an iron fist for decades. The pollution they've caused has devastated the planet, destroying the ozone, and killing off plant and animal life.

Outside of domed cities the air is thin, and the sun scorches all; it's a veritable wasteland. In the past two decades the planet has reached entirely new levels of decay. Extreme weather patterns, and massive quakes, ravage the land.

Time is running out...

Mack and his mercenary troupe set out on a quest to stop the C.D.F.P. once and for all, and the planet will test them to their limits... But are they ready for the horrors they'll uncover? Can they alone stand up against the all-powerful C.D.F.P.?

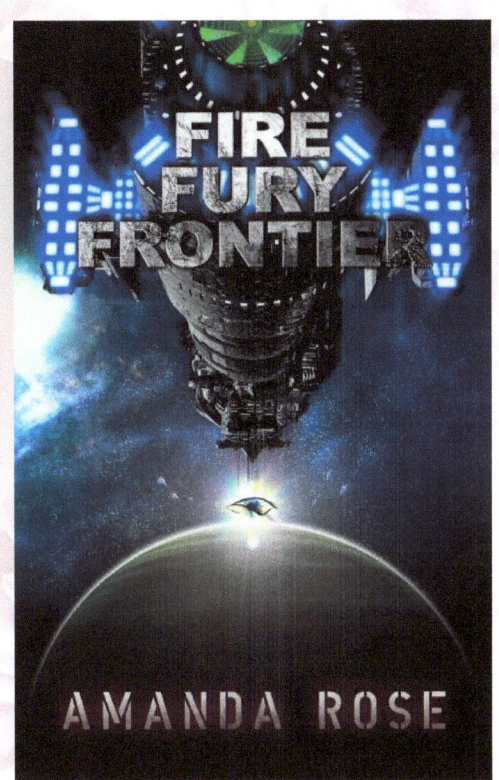

Fire Fury Frontier

Fire Fury Frontier Book Description:

One ship, one last chance to survive...

Humanity's home world has been destroyed from extensive global warming. For over two hundred years the last remaining humans have lived in space aboard a single massive ship, the Saisei. After generations in space, living aboard a ship is all anyone has ever known.

But space is an inhospitable home.

The ship is old and damaged, rations are low, and a planet fit for colonization has never been found.

In the vast expanse of space, as the Saisei makes way to resupply their ship, they stumble upon a discovery that will change the course of human history forever.

ALSO AVAILABLE ON AUDIBLE

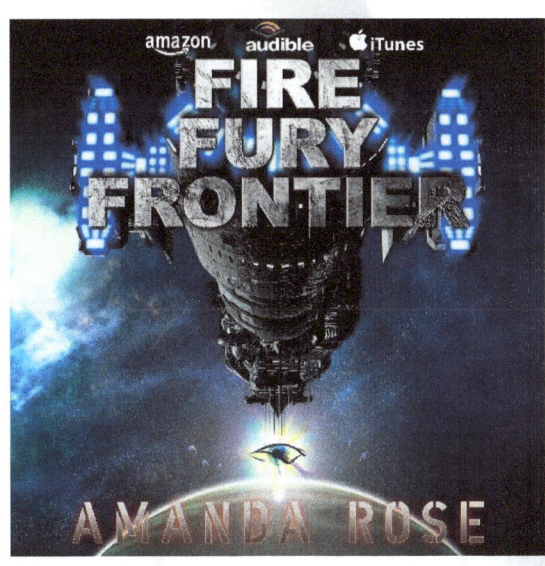

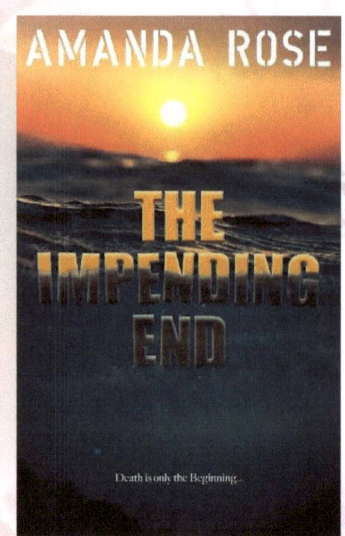

The Impending End

The Impending End Book Description:

It's 2005. Ayla Jefferson is 17, incredibly intelligent, sensitive, imaginative, and thoughtful. She's also contemplating suicide...

After a life long battle with mental illness plaguing her every move, Ayla is ready for death. Eerily calm, she says her goodbyes, and sets out to commit her final act.

But despite her stubborn conviction, life isn't as easy to let go of as she expected. Her hyper-imagination blurs reality and she finds herself getting lost in gripping memories. Mentally disengaged, Ayla's experiences are surreal, and discerning fact from fiction becomes harder and harder.

As the life she's so eager to leave behind begs to hold on, will she be able to leave it all behind?

A Strange Dream: Anthology of Short Stories and Poetry

A Strange Dream Book Description:

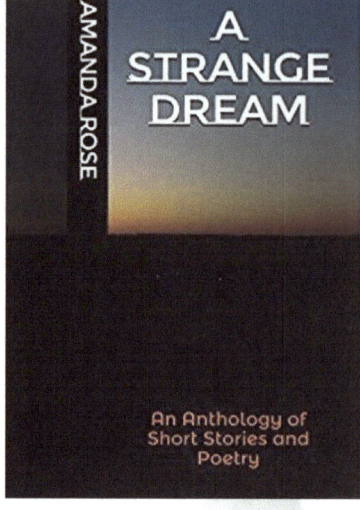

Death, Depression, Insomnia, Prostitution, Eating Disorders, Abortion, Convicts, Insanity, and Marital issues... This anthology of short stories and poetry explores the dark reaches of the mind and mental health issues.

The 9 short stories, including award winning EGGS and OUTSIDER, as well as runner up in the Canadian Writer's Guild Short Prose competition, DROWNING IN SILENCE, and 9 poems, take us on a journey from the surreal to the mundane. From day-to-day life to fantasy, the characters and situations explore many walks of life.

www.ingramcontent.com/pod-product-compliance
Lightning Source LLC
Chambersburg PA
CBHW051027180526
45172CB00002B/499